U.S. Navy SEALs

by Tom Streissguth

Capstone Press

MINNEAPOLIS

Capstone Press • 2440 Fernbrook Lane • Minneapolis, MN 55447

Editorial Director   John Coughlan
Managing Editor   Tom Streissguth
Production Editor   Jim Stapleton
Book Designer   Timothy Halldin

Library of Congress Cataloging-in-Publication Data
Streissguth, Thomas, 1958-
   U. S. Navy SEALs / by Tom Streissguth.
      p. cm. -- (Serving your country)
   Includes bibliographical references (p. 46) and index.
   Summary: Traces the history of this special forces
unit,the training its members must undergo, and its
deployment in modern conflicts.
   ISBN 1-56065-282-9
   1. United States. Navy. SEALs--Juvenile literature.
   2. United States. Navy--Commando troops--Juvenile
literature. [1. United States. Navy. SEALs. 2. United
States Navy--Commando troops.]
   I. Title. II. Series.
   VG87.S74 1996
   359.9--dc20   95-441
                                            CIP
                                             AC

00 99 98 97   8 7 6 5 4 3 2

Table of Contents

Chapter 1

The Story of a SEAL

From the side of your landing craft, you spot a quiet beach in the distance. A strong current is pushing your boat towards the beach. Heavy waves swell underneath and roll towards the rocks on shore.

You're part of a special military unit that has been fighting on land and sea since the early 1960s. Tomorrow, an invasion will hit this beach. But before that happens, your team must swim to shore, clear the beach of mines

The members of the Navy's SEAL teams are well-equipped and always ready for duty.

Team members have to become experts in handling small boats.

and **obstacles**, and prepare for the landing. And you'll have to do it under the watching eyes of the enemy.

It's one of the most dangerous jobs on earth, but your team can handle this mission. You and the other members have been through six months of hard training to prepare. You can swim several miles, handle heavy equipment in the water, and set explosive charges. You also have experience in deep-sea diving and high-altitude parachuting. And you're in top physical condition.

You have to volunteer for this job, and not many volunteers make it. In fact, there's nothing tougher in the U.S. military than this training course. But once you've been through it, you can join a force with a long history and a bright future–the U.S. Navy SEALs.

They move easily from water to land during dangerous operations.

Chapter 2

The History of the SEALs

In December 1941, the Japanese attacked Pearl Harbor, a U.S. naval base in Hawaii. The next day, the United States was at war. The nation was soon fighting Germany as well as Japan. U.S. troops saw action in Europe, North Africa, and on the islands of the Pacific Ocean.

During World War II, the armed forces made many invasions of enemy territory by sea. But

A SEAL team handles a rubber boat as part of their training at Coronado, near San Diego.

A team heads for shore with weapons at the ready.

the invading soldiers often faced land mines, sniper fire, and other dangers. In 1943, the U.S. Navy recruited special teams of experts to clear the beaches before these attacks. These teams were called Naval Combat Demolition Units.

During an invasion, the six-man teams went ashore on the first landing boats. Their job was to clear a path for the coming wave of marines. They scouted enemy positions and marked the safe paths through the water to the beach.

Hard Training

Before joining the teams, the men went through training at Fort Pierce, a military base in Florida. They had to swim, run, and carry heavy loads in all kinds of weather. They practiced with small landing boats and learned how to handle explosives.

Later, the Navy set up new, 100-man squads known as Underwater Demolition Teams, or UDTs. The UDTs took part in all the major landings in the Pacific. Just before the invasion,

SEAL units are trained for careful landings and pickups using a single helicopter line.

they swam ashore, sometimes under heavy fire. Their mission was to set explosive charges on enemy obstacles. After setting the charges, they swam back to their ships. The charges would go off just as the main landing wave was arriving on the beach.

Modified dune buggies carry SEAL teams across rough and sandy terrain and behind enemy lines.

All the time they spent in the water earned the UDT men a nickname–frogmen. By the end of the war in 1945, there were 34 UDT teams, and about 3,400 frogmen, operating in the Pacific Ocean.

Korea and Vietnam

The Korean War broke out in the early 1950s. The UDT teams were back in action. But their mission had changed. They traveled behind enemy lines to destroy bridges, tunnels, railroads, and other important targets. They also became **paratroopers**–soldiers who used parachutes to land from the air.

In the early 1960s, the United States and the Soviet Union were fighting a Cold War. These two "superpowers" weren't actually shooting at each other. But their smaller allies were involved in conflicts all over the world. North Vietnam, for example, was a Soviet ally that was fighting South Vietnam, which was allied with the United States.

President John Kennedy wanted the military to form small teams of **guerrilla** fighters to help America's allies. The U.S. Army already had a special forces unit, nicknamed the Green Berets. In January 1962, the Navy started its own special forces. It was called SEALs–for Sea, Air, and Land teams.

The SEALs in Action

The SEALs grew out of the Navy's UDT teams. Both types of units were called into action during the 1960s, when the United States began sending troops to attack Communist guerrillas. These guerrillas were fighting to overthrow South Vietnam.

The Vietnam War was a hard-fought guerrilla combat. Much of the conflict took place along rivers and streams in the midst of a dense tropical forest. It was the perfect theater of operations for the Navy's elite SEAL teams.

During the 1960s and early 1970s, SEAL teams fought in the dense rain forests of Vietnam.

SEAL units operated along the coasts and rivers of Vietnam. The teams had a very dangerous mission: to disrupt enemy operations behind the lines. The SEAL team members used special riverboats to ambush Communist fighters. They captured prisoners and carried out raids on enemy camps. They

The care and use of weapons is an important part of military training.

sabotaged ammunition dumps, destroyed food stores, and cut enemy communications.

The SEAL teams were among the most effective fighting units of the war. Despite their success, the U.S. and South Vietnam were not able to defeat the Communist guerrillas. The SEALs and the rest of the U.S. military withdrew from the country, and South Vietnam fell to the North.

The U.S. military went through many important changes after the end of the Vietnam War. Many special forces units were deactivated–closed down. Others had to make do with less money. Some military leaders felt there was no longer any need for special forces groups.

Others disagreed. They pointed out that the world's most powerful nations could no longer fight world wars without risking their own survival. Instead, many modern wars are fought by smaller nations, who are supplied by their larger and more powerful allies. Often, these wars involve lightly armed guerrilla forces.

Early naval demolition experts–frogmen–spent most of their time in the water.

Mobility and training are important for guerrilla operations. SEAL teams can train foreign units for their work. They are also ready at all times to carry out guerrilla operations anywhere in the world.

The world was also facing a new kind of war—the fight against terrorism. To frighten nations into meeting their demands, terrorists were hijacking airplanes, attacking civilians, and bombing cities throughout the world. To fight this threat, the United States set up several special anti-terrorism squads. SEAL Team Six is one of these elite units.

During the 1980s, the U.S. military created a new organization of special forces. This was the Special Operations Command, headquartered in Tampa. The Special Operations Command now leads the Navy SEALs, the Green Berets, and all other special forces. The units are fully equipped, well-trained, and prepared. When the United States needs a special mission carried out anywhere in the world, the units of the Special Operations Command will be ready.

The use of weapons and explosives is a part of all special forces training.

Chapter 3
SEAL Training

Y ou have to serve in the United States
Navy in order to become a SEAL. And the
SEAL teams take only volunteers–those who
ask to join. Before you are assigned to a SEAL
team, you must go through Basic Underwater
Demolition/Seal training, or BUDS. This
training takes place at the Naval Special
Warfare Center at Coronado, a base in southern
California on the Pacific Ocean.

**SEAL teams have to be ready for swimming under
water and under difficult conditions.**

In this exercise, divers must retrieve face masks with their hands tied.

BUDS Training

The BUDS training begins with nine weeks of hard physical exercise. Trainees must run long distances over land and swim up to two miles in the open sea. They learn how to use swimming gear, how to rescue swimmers in trouble, and how to safely jump into open water from a helicopter. Every day, they do lots of calisthenics–jumping jacks, pushups, pullups, situps, and other exercises.

Instructors push the trainees as hard as they can. They are often shouting orders, encouragement, criticism, and directions all at once. The instructors have to be in good shape. During PT–physical training–they do everything that the trainees have to do.

BUDS training tests volunteers with difficult tasks–some of them done under water.

Working Together

The instructors assign each trainee a swim buddy. The two men must train together all the time. In this way, future SEALs learn to never leave a teammate behind–and the SEALs have never left a team member to be taken prisoner in combat.

The trainees also form teams. They learn to help each other, and they learn to depend on each other. The instructor may command six of

SEAL teams always work together. Members never train by themselves.

Doing push-ups in the pounding surf is one of the easier parts of Hell Week.

them to carry a heavy log through pounding surf. Or the trainees may have to carry a heavy rubber raft up a steep sand dune. Some men are stronger than others, but all the members of a team need to finish the task together.

The instructors know that in a real war, the members of a SEAL team will have to rely on each other to carry out their mission. It is very likely that they will be working and fighting far from any outside help. Their lives will depend on good teamwork.

A Tough Week

The sixth week of training is a very difficult test that all candidates for the Navy SEALs fear. The instructors call it Motivation Week, but trainees have a much stronger name for it–Hell Week.

During Hell Week, instructors push trainees to their limit, and then push them even more. The instructors shout commands over a megaphone while shells explode nearby. Trainees run, crawl, do push-ups, scramble over obstacle courses, and sweat. They sit in cold, pounding surf with their arms linked with other team members. They spend 15 minutes in the water, then 5 minutes out of the water, over and over again.

The trainees must do constant physical exercise and difficult team missions. They run miles over deep sand and spend hours in a deep mud pit. For the entire week, they are allowed only a small amount of sleep.

After Hell Week, there are three more weeks of physical training, followed by diving instruction.

Scuba Training

For seven weeks, the BUDS trainees learn how to use **scuba** gear. Scuba stands for Self-Contained Underwater Breathing Apparatus.

Underwater training takes up many important weeks of the BUDS training course.

The gear includes an air tank, a regulator to control the flow of air, a breathing tube, and a mask. Since the early 1950s, scuba gear has helped divers to spend long periods of time underwater.

BUDS trainees first learn basic diving techniques. They begin in a swimming pool, spending a few minutes underwater each time. They learn how to breathe, how to swim, and how to clear a mask of water. They also learn the proper way to swim from deep underwater

Navy powerboats speed a SEAL team toward shore.

back to the surface. Later, they practice in the open ocean. The cold water and high waves of the ocean make scuba training much more difficult.

After scuba diving, trainees enter the third and final phase of training. An important part of this phase is work with demolitions–the science of explosives. Instructors show the different kinds of explosives, and how strong a charge is needed to destroy a bridge, a building, or a boat.

Trainees learn how to handle explosives and how to guard against booby traps. By the end of the course, they will be able to clear mines from beaches. They also know first aid.

Cast and Recovery

Trainees then practice the basic missions of a UDT team. To prepare for seaborne invasions, they make landings on a rocky beach and in high surf. During the landing, they must leap out of a rubber boat and hide it out of sight above the surf line. They must be careful not to be crushed by the pounding waves.

Trainees climb into a speeding motorboat during cast-and-recovery operations.

Another important part of this training is cast-and-recovery. Wearing scuba gear, trainees ride in a landing craft that is tied to a rubber boat. On a signal from the instructor, they jump one by one into the boat and then into the surf.

After a short time, the boat returns to recover divers at the right pickup spots. A member of the boat crew extends a rubber loop towards the divers in the water. The divers must

A boat crew collects trainees after an exercise in the waters off San Diego.

grasp the loop and pull themsleves into the boat.

The BUDS teams also use helicopters for these cast-and-recovery operations. The divers must jump into the water from the helicopter, then catch a line to return.

To prepare for future missions, instructors teach **land navigation**, the use of climbing ropes, and infantry tactics. Trainees spend four weeks practicing infantry skills on San Clemente Island, off the California coast.

Jump Training

The future Navy SEALs then learn to parachute at the U.S. Army Airborne School at Fort Benning, Georgia. First they make **static line** jumps, in which a line pulls open the parachute as they jump from the plane. Then they learn to free fall, to make high-altitude jumps, and to jump into different kinds of terrain and open water.

After finishing the basic course, the Navy assigns the men to either a UDT team or a SEAL team, depending on the need. SEAL members must go through a six-month probation period. If they fail to live up to SEAL standards, they are reassigned.

The BUDS course takes 25 weeks. More than half of the volunteers drop out before the end of the course. Those who make it may join one of the best-trained units in the armed forces–the U.S. Navy SEALs.

Chapter 4

A Mission in Kuwait

The Persian Gulf War began in January 1991. For a month, U.S. aircraft bombed cities and military bases in Iraq. By late February, the United States and its allies were ready to move into Kuwait, the small nation that Iraq had invaded and occupied in the summer of 1990. It was now time for the ground war.

A powerful force of tanks, artillery, and infantry prepared to cross the Iraqi lines. The United States also moved several units of Navy ships off the coast of Kuwait. Aboard these ships were thousands of U.S. Marines, equipped for a landing. But the marines weren't going ashore. Instead, the plan was to trick the Iraqis into preparing for a seaborne invasion–then attacking by land. To carry out the plan, the military called on the Navy SEALs.

Camouflage is a common part of guerrilla warfare, no matter what the terrain may be like.

A Dangerous Mission

On the night of February 23, a team of six Navy SEALs started out on their mission. They raced along the shore of Kuwait in two Fountain-33 speedboats. Still several miles from shore, they climbed into landing boats and headed for the beach.

Still 500 yards out, the team slipped over the sides of their craft. They swam toward shore with heavy packs of explosives strapped

to their bodies. To fool the Iraqis into thinking landing craft were approaching, they set out marker buoys in the water.

Finally, the team scrambled up the beach. They set the charges in their backpacks to explode at exactly 1 a.m. They placed the charges, then headed back for the open water. The ground war was scheduled to begin just a few hours later.

After swimming back to their boats, the SEAL team opened fire with machine guns and set more explosive charges off in the water. The shore explosives made a tremendous noise and a bright light. The SEAL team sped away.

Soon the radios of the Iraqi forces were busy with shouting and orders. The Iraqi generals ordered two **divisions** to move away from the front lines. They sped to the east, and toward the beaches of Kuwait City. But they would find only sand and water. Early the next day, the Allied ground invasion of Iraq and Kuwait began.

Chapter 5

If You Want to Join the SEALs

Volunteers for the U.S. Navy must be at least 17 years old. A high-school diploma is not necessary, but those who don't have one will not be able to attend many courses and schools that the Navy offers.

During basic training, **enlistees** may volunteer for the Navy's Special Warfare Program. They may also volunteer at any time during their service, provided they are 28 years old or younger.

SEALS must be excellent swimmers, must have good hearing and vision, and must be ready for difficult physical challenges. Because the SEALs are a combat unit, the Navy will not accept women as SEAL volunteers.

All SEAL volunteers should be in good physical condition before they begin the course. To prepare, the Navy asks trainees to run 15 miles a week, swim for 60 minutes without stopping, and lift weights three days a week. A physical fitness test for volunteers includes swimming, push-ups, sit-ups, chinups, and running. A good previous record in the Navy is also required.

Glossary

division–a large military unit

enlistee–someone who volunteers for military service.

guerrilla–a soldier who fights on his own or with a small, loosely organized force

land navigation–the task of finding one's way across unmarked terrain

obstacle–something that blocks a path

paratroopers–soldiers who parachute into battle

sabotage–destruction of enemy property

scuba–breathing equipment for underwater diving

static line–a device that opens a parachute automatically as the jumper leaves the plane

To Learn More

King, John. *The Gulf War.* New York: Dillon Press, 1991.

Macdonald, Robert W. *Exploring Careers in the Military Services.* New York: The Rosen Publishing Group, 1991.

Naden, Corinne J. and Rose Blue. *The U.S. Navy.* Brookfield, CT: Millbrook Press, 1993.

Pelta, Kathy. *The U.S. Navy.* Minneapolis: Lerner Publications.

Some Useful Addresses

UDT/ SEAL Museum
3300 A1A Highway
Ft. Pierce, FL 33450

Naval Special Warfare Center
Naval Amphibious Base
Coronado
San Diego, CA 92118

Navy-Marine Corps ROTC College
  Scholarship Program
801 N. Randolph St.
Arlington, VA 22203

Index